Mabel D Sand

CHAUCER

THE LESLIE STEPHEN LECTURE

Spoken at Cambridge, March 2, 1931

CHAUCER

BY

JOHN MASEFIELD

NEW YORK

THE MACMILLAN COMPANY

1931

PRINTED IN THE UNITED STATES OF AMERICA
BY THE FERRIS PRINTING COMPANY

CHAUCER

CHAUCER

I AM to talk to you for an hour about Geoffrey Chaucer, the first of the three great English poets. An hour isn't very long to give to the life's work of a great man. And an hour's prose about poetry will not take you very far, for how shall prose illuminate poetry?

I am not learned, and therefore do not know all the elements in Chaucer's mind. Much in him does not interest me. Boëthius doesn't console me, and I have small patience with an astrolabe. I think that some of Chaucer belongs to his time and that much of that time is dead, extinct, and never to be made alive again. What was alive in it, lives through him.

I must say a few words about the England of his time. It was a sparsely populated country with much marsh and waste and forest. When he was a little boy the great pestilence of bubonic plague, the Black Death, came here, and destroyed as some think, one person in every four or five. This was an exceptional

Death, but pestilence was here in every year of his life, and thrice in his life was very mortal. The cities were walled and ditcht about: they contained a few churches and palaces of delicate beauty and many rat-ridden lousy hovels. Men carried weapons and often used them: streets were dangerous with brawls: fires were very destructive, water being so scarce. There was much squalor, dirt, degradation and ignorance, out of which life grew turbulently upon a sturdy stock.

You could walk out of London in a quarter of an hour, into country, little fenc't, hardly draind, scarcely farmd, save in the old Common Field system. You were guided from settlement to settlement by the roofs, spires or bell-towers of the churches. The roads were just tracks, or those left by the Romans 1,000 years before: the stags and the foxes were a sad trouble in many places, quite near to London. Many people everywhere had given up the world for religion: were living in communities to that end. There were no means of getting about save the horse and cart and an odd sort of ship with one mast and sail. But everybody who hadn't died young, or been killed by plague, famine, battle or murder was as tough as oak: indifferent to lice, dirt, cold or heat, and so went wandering unwasht and happy, all over Europe, from shrine to shrine, into odd lands, into heathendom, and got to Jerusalem and often went to Rome and so were a more travelld nation than we are to-day and knew a deal more of the inner lives of the nations with which they mixt.

If a man wanted bread, he got it from a monastery: if he wanted a Circus, he got it in a pageant of the Church, or some savagery of justice. Life being what it was, a man had a good chance of seeing those who differ'd from him in politics or philosophy, hangd drawn and quarterd, burned at stakes or boild in oil.

Something is known of Chaucer's life. He was the son of a London vintner. At an early age he entered Court in the service of King Edward III. He married. He served in the French war, was taken prisoner and ransom'd. He lived at one time at Court, then over one of the city gates, and at another time in Greenwich. As he was known to the King, and probably a good linguist, he was sometimes employd in France and Flanders on missions of trust. He was twice thus in Italy. He was always a scholar and student, a lover of books and of nature, and deeply influenct first by the poetry of France and later by that of Italy. He was rather shy and fat. He was not abstemious. He was twice set upon by robbers and robbed of the King's money. His marriage seems to have been unhappy, and his son is thought to have died before him. He wrote a great many stories of different kinds, most of them in verse, some of them translated from foreign tongues. He was interested in Astronomy and in Judicial Astrology. He was honoured at Court. He was sometimes prosperous and sometimes in want of money. He belonged to a set of people critical of abuses in the Church. The only man who knew him well and wrote about him praises him in terms almost of idolatry. This man also painted a portrait of him. He had the fortune of being very prosperous during the years of his greatest creative power. He died in 1400 aged about 60.

Some of the artists living in England when he was a young man were doing lovely work which has never been surpasst. Some of our builders, carvers, broiderers and metal workers were exquisite masters: but our poets were not masters. In poetry, before Chaucer matured, our achievement was rude and dull.

There was a rude poetry of the people, often moving from its sincerity and force; some of it very precious for its power of shewing us that vanisht England as it was to the poet; it has the quality of earthenware; it is hand-made, and of the hearth, but it could not be exported. There was a considerable mass of religious and improving poetry: there always has been in this land. There were poets writing in Latin and in French: we still have such. There were tellers of tales of adventure, of knights riding forth to fight with giants and pigmies or to love fairy ladies. All of this work, once done with pain by living men, was of use to that age and is now dead. Men print it: men pass examinations in it, but it brings no bread and drink to the soul.

The age in which Chaucer wrote was one of passionate change, of old things coming to an end, and the world being re-born, as it is to-day. New ways of thought were creating new ways of life.

We all have suffer'd from a cold or a fever, which seizes on the body, beats it low, and itself rises and rages, running its course, as we call it, until it dies down, loses virulence and fades from us. It is as though a fungus or parasite had been able to blot us out for a while. We all have known the excitement and obsession of a great event, a contest, dispute, trial or war, how it begins, so often from a small cause, and goes on gathering strength, until it has fann'd all hearts and minds into a passion, which they mistake for fine feeling and wisdom, but later seems neither, but rather folly: and in the fury of this passion what will not men and nations do and say? Then the thing comes to an end, or is flung off, after enough harm has been done, or the fuel is spent: it has been like a fire burning or a disease wasting: a fungus or parasite blotting us out for a while.

Then, as now, a movement for more light was shaking the known world. To-day, we are apt to judge the movement by what is worst in it. We are apt to judge that ancient movement by what was best in it and its results. The brutality, the catchwords, the falsehood and fury of movers and obstructors are now all gone with the waste of time. We know that more light came into the world, mainly thro' a few great men, some of whom being painters and poets, passed their days in the portraying and the telling of stories.

Let me speak to you of Chaucer to-day not as a learned man nor as one interested in the 14th century; but as one fond of stories and interested in all ways of telling them and in all systems of arranging them when told.

People tell stories because they have a genius for it. People listen to stories, because life is so prone to action that the very shadow of action will sway the minds of men and women: any purpose will arrest no purpose.

A story being a work of art must have a beginning, a middle and an end: the clearer the better.

In the beginning, this race did not tell good stories, but made rough statements of fact, such as the entries in the Anglo-Saxon Chronicle:

> This year such an one was King.
> This year much folk died.

Each of these would make the beginning of a tale, like the simple statement: The Rat sat on the Mat.

But if you add to the statement another statement complicating the former you increase the interest,

> The Rat sat on the Mat. The Cat came in.

you bring in anxiety, as to what will happen, and suspense as to how and when. You have now the beginning and the middle of a tale or work of art. If you are one sort of writer you will now end it by saying the Cat killed the Rat. If you are another sort of writer you will say The Rat killed the Cat. If on the other hand you are neither, but only an intellectual, you will say they disagreed.

CHAUCER

The story-teller having thus made his story clear
to himself will see in it opportunities for the emphasis
of certain points, selecting, of course, for emphasis,
those points which are opportunities for his own
genius, whatever that may be: and will endeavour to
apply it to the system of his thoughts of life.

The Homeric poet might use such an incident to
preserve tribal legend.

"Then Rat and Cat strode forward, girded with
    gleaming bronze
And when they were near each other, first Rat
    shouted
'Ho, Trojan Cat, now shall my pitiless spear-point
Tear you, and I will take your armour for mine
And fling your corpse far into eddying Xanthos
For the little fishes and twisting eels to pluck at.'
So saying he hurled his great long-shadowing spear
Nor did he miss, but struck on the bossy shield,
Great, knoppt with silver, bronze-bound, seven bulls'
    hides thick,
Which Ares wrought for Ilos in pleasant Ida,
And Ilos gave it to Phylax who dwelld in Lycia,
By the black-flowing holy waters of far Kayster.
But him the horses of God killed in the mountain,
The golden horses that crop the undying grass
In the glens where the Nymphs go dancing and sing-
    ing songs."

Dante, shall we say, might take the tale as an illus-
tration in some part of his vast system:—

"Within that seventh circle of red hell
There came what seem'd a squeak, and looking near
Lo, a black-visaged Cat, exceeding fell,
Who on the shadow of a Rat made cheer.
Then I, to my sweet Guide, said, 'Master, tell,
If it be not forbidden, what are these
Shades dim as faces not remember'd well?'
Then he to me: 'The active influences
Acquire on the heart good power or bad.
This is the end of too much love of cheese.' "

Or coming nearer home, William Wordsworth might
take the tale and mix it with morality and mountains
in an address to Samuel Taylor Coleridge:

"O Friend, as we descended to our tea
The mountains spoke to us of these high things
And the red sunset sang: deep thoughts were ours
Of Man and Nature: Man's unconquer'd Will
And Nature: topic vast: poetic theme.
When lo, by Wilkinson's green cabbage-plot
A village Idiot Boy, swinging a Rat
Which my Companion's Cat had lately kill'd
Brought sudden horror into both our Minds."

Chaucer's way with a fable, I will speak of later,

when I speak of the two somewhat conflicting currents in his mind. I need only say here that a man states his fable with himself or with what is strongest in himself.

I have spoken, so far, only of Narrative. As you all know:

There is a simpler way of stating the fable: it does not concern us, but it is a great way. The dramatic way. Curtain rising discovers Rat. Enter Cat.

Pounce. Ow! Curtain.

There are many mixtures of the two methods, and countless varieties of both. In rare ages of time rare souls use the methods with such imaginative power that what is eternally True in life is apprehended and made apparent to us, in images of beauty and joy and vigour. These images are the only reality known to us here on earth. Beside them, living persons seem shadows.

We, now, are not in one of those rare ages, but may perhaps be stumbling and struggling towards the preparation of one.

⸸ We do not use either method with imaginative power, but we use them both for our amusement as freely as any age that ever was. On this day, ten works of fiction are being publisht: and to-morrow ten more will be publisht, in this land alone: for ten a day appear each year, life is never so interesting that fiction cannot charm. Some tale of an unreal world is always wanted: to create it is such rapture and to read it such fun.

Chaucer was born into an age as greedy of tales as this age. He was born with a rare aptness for the telling of tales, and with a greedy fondness for them. A story and leave to tell a story were what he most wanted from life. To read and to tell stories made up that Law of his Being, which men of genius obey.

The problems: what made a tellable tale for his mood at the time: and how to tell the tale chosen were the main concerns of his art. All through his life, his leisure was given to the study of stories and to attempts to tell them.

Some people to-day wonder why he did not tell the tales in prose: well, sometimes he did; and those who read his tales in prose will perhaps be thankful that it was not his usual practice. But still, the question is askt to-day: it is often askt, by those who do not care for verse, why all tales are not in prose?

Chaucer wrote in verse because he preferred verse to prose.

He preferred verse to prose for many reasons, of

which I will mention these: because when his tales were as he tells us "said, or ellës sung," the beat of the rhythm made an excitement in his hearers, and in that excitement they could the better perceive what he had seen.

Then his subjects were poetical: they were of the imagination and demanded the language of the imagination.

Sometimes, he was writing of events so great and of people so beautiful, strong and generous, that the language and the rhythms of daily life were insufficient to describe them. They could only be described in the language of deep feeling. The people who could neither be excited by that feeling nor kindled by that depth and generosity of language were not his concern. He was addressing those in whom was the substance of life.

Sometimes, he was writing of events which were not great, and of people who were loud and lusty, in merry and bawdy situations. Here again the language and the rhythms of daily life were insufficient to describe them. As in the former case his concern was to give Beauty, so, in this case, his concern was to give Life, to strip his characters and situations down to their Realities, and to make his statement of them intense and living, to burn away and hammer out everything that was not in character and in keeping, to make one see the place and to see and hear the people; and to do this, while telling the merry tale, cannot be done in prose; poetry only can give that concentrated intensity. . . .

But all these poetical powers were wanting to the young Chaucer. To begin with he was, as I have said, a man greedy of tales and with an aptness for telling them; as we should say he was fond of literature and had a bent towards narrative. But he had as yet no power of narrative, no power of any sort, just a liking for poetry and a weak grace of imitation. If in his maturity, 45 or so, he was, as he says, shy and not prone to enter into talk, he was probably shyer as a lad. It is quite plain that he did not begin to learn his craft as a story-teller by telling his tales by word of mouth. Had he done so, he would have attained a skill in story-telling much more quickly than he did. But even had he longed to tell his tales aloud there was as yet no measure in English in which he could tell them. He was in the cultivated Court, where men were speaking, reading and writing French. If they read the English verse of the time they probably thought it rude, and condemned its measures as barbarous. The jingling, the ballade, and the alliterative English measures were of the people, not of the Court. Throughout his life Chaucer only once, so far as we know, used one of these three measures and then only to mock it. He once mentions the alliterative measure, but never uses it.

His early work is not that of a creator, but of an imitator, or sensitive scholar trying to attain skill in writing by imitating whatever examples of it he could find in the work of the French poets then being read at Court. The English which was then coming into use at Court was full of French forms and words which have now ceast to be in English use. He therefore probably found it much easier to adapt the French verse-forms to English use than we should find it to-day: the tongues fitted more closely.

As a beginner, he turned, as beginners usually will, to the men who did easily and gracefully what he longed to do. He turned especially to the lyrical poems of a French poet Machault, who wrote skilfully in ways not practist in English. The forms used by Machault were usually ballades of three 8-line stanzas followed by a quatrain.

He also used a rhymed couplet of ten-syllabled

lines, and a variant from the ballade in which each stanza contained only seven lines. Chaucer practist the 8-line ballade form with some success; and got a certain skill from it. He practist the rhymed couplet of ten-syllabled lines, and saw at once its use and its limitations. He also turned to the 7-line stanza, and returned to it. Machault had not used it in any poem that was not trifling. Chaucer found it a very handy form, with this great merit that none of its rhyme-sounds is repeated more than thrice. In a language like English, with so few rhymes, this is a great boon. Chaucer saw that it was a verse-form fairly easy to write, simple and pleasant to speak and beautiful to listen to. Being himself a story-teller rather than a writer of trifles, he tried it in Narrative, and found that a story could be told in it. Later in life he used it repeatedly and in some of his most successful tales. It is one of the most useful and beautiful of common English verse-forms. It is far better suited to Narrative than the more complex and more difficult Spenserian stanza which some later poets, writing for a reading public, have preferr'd.

It is so linkt with Chaucer, that many of you will know the verse-form as "Chaucerian stanza" or "Cressid verse." Later, when King James of Scotland wrote the *Kingis Quair* in it, some people called it Rhyme Royal. But it is Chaucer's stanza. He took it from a fifth-rate poet who did not see what could be done with it, and used it for the first time in English in important poems. It will probably be used in English for some centuries to come: it is Chaucer's great contribution to our ways of writing.

While he was in this period of French influence, he read the strange, beautiful and somewhat bitter French poetical *Romance of the Rose*. This swayed and formed his mind as profoundly as Machault had formed his manner. He tells us that he translated it. That part of the translation which has survived is a work of sensitive, delicate, accurate skill. No poem influenct him more deeply. It is no longer new to the world: it has been often imitated: and the world's tastes have changed: but once it was new, even to-day when a lad comes to it for the first time, in the early days of his reading, the opening is a doorway into a new world of beauty and strangeness. It is a doorway through which a reader can pass into a world of the imagination eternally and untellably beautiful.

Think what it must have been to a young poet who had read few poems and none in the least like this, to read for the first time of one coming with an ecstasy of expectation to strange walls upon which all the evil and hateful and painful things are wrought: and then, passing within those walls into a marvellous garden: and then, within the garden, meeting with marvellous persons: and always having the feeling that the dream is going to become Vision, that is Eternal, True, Joyous and Wise.

What happens is not Vision, and to us, in this state of the world, it is not joyous nor wise. Instead of the mysteries and raptures of love there is moral homily mixt with a little social satire. It is like going to Twickenham to see an International Match and there being lecturd on the Moral Aspects of Football. However, the homily and the satire when they were new went into the hearts of that time.

This poem was the mould in which Chaucer's mind was cast. In the end, as he went on coining, his mind broke the mould: it was too narrow for him. But a sort of flavour or memory or ghost of that poem is in his very best work until the end: Some of the very best of him, as always happens, is due to what was undying in his master.

These French influences gave him form and subject, with which he struggled for some years, his main interest being always the telling of tales. The early tales are all marred by literature and artifice. He could not make his fables simple.

Following the example of the *Romance of the Rose,* he would begin with a dream, and then pass into a description, and then meet a god or an allegorical figure or one of the Virtues, who would take him somewhere else so that he could describe it: and having gone so far his young brain was tired and the original mood was gone, and his fable in such a mess that nothing could make it either coherent or effective in spite of the grace and colour and liveliness of some of the writing. Those three qualities of grace, colour and liveliness were always there, for the first time in English poetry. The poems are charming, in thought and feeling, even if they are weak in design. They are full of fresh, clear, vivid images, sharp in outline, bright in colour. They are also lively: the birds and allegorical figures talk pointedly and delightfully: and one meets with Chaucer's pleasant humour, which is so shrewd, charming and fresh. Images and allegorical figures had been known before: they were part of poetry's stock-in-trade, but humour of this sort was a new thing in poetry.

Chaucer had been living for some years under the

eye of the King. When he was about thirty years of age he was sent to Italy upon a Mission, rode there overland, did his work and rode back. In Italy, he may have met Petrarch; in any case he met the Renaissance in its flowering, and saw works of great and confident design carried to splendid completion. He saw what Art could be under the influence of the Sun, and read some of the long narrative poems of Boccaccio, and felt a power everywhere about him far greater than the fantasies of the *Romance of the Rose*.

On his return, he was given some work in the London Customs House and a lodging over Aldgate. This lodging over a city gate was well-built and well-guarded, which few city houses were: it had a certain privacy about it; and at the same time a view of town and country, and of busy life. One great drawback was that like other city gates it was a sort of museum of the heads, arms and legs of traitors, set up there on iron spikes after execution. It was in this lodging over Aldgate, when not working in the Customs, that Chaucer wrote his first long poem, the novel in verse, of *Troilus and Cressida*, founded on Boccaccio's long poem, *Il Filostrato*.

The story is this: Troilus in the City of Troy falls

in love with Cressida, whose uncle, Pandarus, makes the two acquainted. They become lovers, but behave more like simple friends or lunatics. Towards the end, Cressida leaves Troy, with vows of constancy which she breaks. Troilus watches for her in vain: she does not come back: he finds his love-token on the body of a captive Greek and knows that she has forsaken him. After some time of bitterness he is killed in battle, and as a blissful ghost he rises above the world and surveys it and laughs at his old sorrow.

Chaucer made the tale for the effect of the climax, which is beautiful. On the way to his climax, he found room for many things besides, and wrought them to the full. The tale is ample, roomy and leisurely; there are these things in it: First, the image of Troy, the first image of Troy in English poetry, and by much the best constructed. It is a real city, based no doubt on 14th-century London, clearly seen and described from whatever point was needed. Next, for the first time in English, the characters are made real: they have lives and passions of their own which make us feel for them. Then, as in the earlier and slighter poems, there are abundant decorations of lively and sweet description, graces of thought and feeling, and that fresh wise shrewd

CHAUCER

humour which blesses so much of what he did.
There are several interruptions to the tale, including
a discussion of Free Will which seems to have long
perplext him: but the tale holds the reader, by itself,
as well as by Chaucer's charm; and at the end of the
six or seven hours which it takes to read, it sways the
reader deeply as it swayed Chaucer. It was a bold and
new experiment by a young man feeling for power
and for style: it had the effect of most bold and new
experiments by young men: it rousd a pretty scandal.
Here was a poet telling a long story with an unhappy
end, in violation of the laws of art, and with an in-
constant lady in it, in defiance of the laws of nature
and morality.

The tale however had one quality which was not
in the critics' books of rules: it was alive: and this
quality of life is often the English contribution.

The writing of a long work is often helpful to a
writer, for mental growth comes with effort. The
writing of *Troilus and Cressida* helpt Chaucer's
growth in several ways. It gave him a power of con-
trol over his table. He drove his resty and unruly
team of lovers over a perplexing course, held them
well together, and made a good finish. He also
seems to have learn'd that that kind of story, of

[21]

strongly imagin'd characters, in romantic relationships, which had won Italy, was too long for his own purposes. It is a long work, which would take six or seven hours to read aloud, and of course many days to copy. Something within himself, and perhaps within his audience, warned him to be briefer henceforth. He attempted no other tale in verse of similar length. As a rule his stories take in the telling less than an hour: only two of the verse tales take a great deal longer.

After writing *Troilus* the influence of Italy remained strongly upon him. The long, stirring poems of Boccaccio with their boldly marshalld fables, rousing rhetoric and romantic people put all other poems out of his mind for the time. But beside these poems, there was in his mind the image of the romantic Italy which had produced them. A brightness of remember'd splendour comes into all his best work after his visit to Italy. He was to go there again before he died and fill his mind with her images of overwhelming vitality.

And at this point, I want to speak to you of a problem which besets all English writers of merit. We stand mid-way between the North, from which our peoples come, and the South, where the Sun shines and Art is gracious. The instinct of the North is for honest, accurate portrayal of person, country and event. The typical artists of the North are Holbein, Rembrandt, the English portrait and landscape-painters, and the makers of the Sagas. Their work is all faithful, sterling and stern. It is noble and truthful. You can reverence and respect it, but it is not charming nor is it splendid.

In the South, in Italy and Greece where the Sun shines, the instinct is for grace and splendour of life: whenever religion and politics permit, the arts flourish so beautifully and naturally that they seem to come like breathing. In the warmth, gaiety and radiance of the Sun, marvellous works are created. The artists of our race, looking upon these marvellous works, are beset with a problem:—Is not this marvellous, sunny art a thing to follow and to imitate? Is it not the only real Art? Is not our own truthful and honest delineation merely a low realism?

Some hesitate; the weak ones imitate; and the strongest are influenced, though sometimes with the feeling that in their concessions they are false to their own genius, which is of the North.

This problem came poignantly to Chaucer when his great gifts were in their fullest maturity. It is

Samuel's problem: Hath the Lord as great delight in burnt offerings and sacrifices as in obeying the voice of the Lord?

Behold, to obey is better than sacrifice and to hearken than the fat of rams.

Much of Chaucer's mind was in a ferment of admiration for the work of French and Italian poets and for the glory in Italy: a full half of all his energy went to shew this admiration. But the other half of all his energy was true to his own so different genius: it was in rebellion against France and Italy: and telling him that his own gift was not and could not be an exulting in the glory of thought, but a lively portrayal of the life about him by his own shrewd and humorous sense of character. To any one of the world poets whom he so revered:—

"Virgile, Ovyde, Omer, Lucan, Stace"

the work of his own native genius might not seem to be poetry, nor even in any way a work of art. None the less his marching and working word was

"Let thy gost thee lead
And Trouthe shal delivre hit is no drede."

His one original work, by which he comes to life as a creator, the maker of a new thing, was done, surely, in revolt from those foreign glories. He turned from them and entered the abundance of his own self, because the World of Art excluded this world of living people, which interested him so deeply.

He may also have felt that the tales from France and Italy, upon which he had workt for so long, could not become his till he had put them in a framework entirely his, which owed nothing to any foreign master.

He set down a scheme or image of the England that he knew, simplified to its elements. He displayed the significant figures of the time in their habits and their natures, with their jealousies, franknesses, and generosities, in a way of his own. He planned to display these significant figures as bound together by the common purpose of a Pilgrimage to Canterbury, and moving on, telling stories by the way, until each had told two tales on the road to Canterbury and two more on the road back to London, where the tales were to be judged at a supper before the company scatterd.

The company of pilgrims had been formed, we are not told how, before Chaucer joined them at the Tabard Tavern in Southwark. There were twenty-nine of them, of whom twenty are described carefully. The company is made up to thirty by Chaucer and to thirty-one by the Host of the Tavern, Harry Baily, who is not described but created as an image of coarse forceful rough capacity and power. On the road, two more join the company, one of whom stays for only a little while.

Of the company, one member in every three is in the service of the Church, either actively as the Persone, or in contemplation, like the Nuns and the Prioress. Reckoning that ten of the society are in religion; three are concernd with the raising of food; another three seem to be mainly occupied with wool; two with war, two with foreign trade, two are in learned professions, the rest are followers of the crafts necessary to man in all ages, the Cook, the Miller, etc.

There is no married couple in the company, nor any young unmarried woman not in religion, there is only one young man. If Chaucer were to write his tales now, of people going on pilgrimage to Saint Ski in winter, or the blissful Lido in the summer, how differently the company would be composed: One person in religion, five in learned professions, with their wives, fifteen young unmarried women and the rest yonge squiers.

Of the two women in the company whom Chaucer describes, one afterwards describes herself, her inclinations and her past with a frankness so full that quieter ages can but wonder. This Wife of Bath was, as she says, one in whom Venus and Mars were strongly and well-aspected in her horoscope. The poems lead us to guess that Mars was unfortunate and Venus depresst in Chaucer's own horoscope.

We gather from the poems that Chaucer's own marriage was one of the utmost and liveliest unfortunate horror.

The Wife of Bath describes her fifth marriage as being to much such a Clerk as Chaucer's description of himself.

Can it possibly be that the Wife of Bath is a portrait of Mrs Chaucer?

With this mixt assembly Chaucer could stand as a portrayer of the time, as well as a teller of tales. In his prologue and in the accounts of what was said and done between the stories, he describes the natures of his chief characters: the tale each tells is in accord with the nature.

He contrives that the noble tale, what he calls the "storial thing that toucheth gentillesse" more than holds the balance with the bold bawdy commonness of his churls. There are the two types of tale, one from the Human Imagination of the complete being, the other from the Animal Imagination of the natural man. The concept of the two bound together upon a pilgrimage is that of a great poet, summing up the Middle Ages. The variant from that concept, that of Cervantes, is that of a great Renaissance gentleman mocking the Middle Ages.

Apart from the beauty and the power of the concept, Chaucer is a master story-teller in at least a dozen stories: that is, he can hold an audience by the interest of his fable, surprise them by the depth and purity of his sincerity, which speaks from the very heart of his imagined character, win them by living description, and fill their World of Imagination with persons of force and fury, and others of beauty and gentleness.

You must read the stories: it is not for me who am a story-teller to spoil your joy in them by telling you all about them. Of the gentle tales I like best *The Knight's Tale*. It is mainly adapted from Boccaccio, but Chaucer's work upon it is that of a master. Next to this, I put the narrative parts of the *Pardoner's Tale;* and then the beautiful tale of the *Franklin*. Of these three tales from the countries of the Sun, one is from Italy, one from France, the third, perhaps, from India.

To these tales, I add one or two of the tragical tales told by the Monk, especially that vigorous tale of Croesus.

Of the simple, English tales, I like best the *Reeve's* and the *Miller's*. I have often deeply regretted that the *Cook's* was never finisht.

But Chaucer himself was finisht before he had written more than about a fifth part of what he had planned to do. *The Canterbury Tales* are unfinisht, even some of the tales which have surviv'd are unfinisht. He left more incomplete work behind him than any other great English poet. It would be interesting to know why. Was it some failure of strength, or purpose; want of leisure and opportunity; the pressure of public service; or lack of encouragement; or all these things acting together? In the end of the *Persone's Tale* there is printed a sad paragraph of repentance for much of his work. It is supposed that he wrote this in sickness shortly before his death. I hope that this paragraph is a forged interpolation. But in any case let us ignore it. We all know man's weakness, we all suffer from it. But the great man's strength is the important thing. In his strength Chaucer was the first of our three great poets, the creator of a method and of a system. No other English poet, except Milton, added so much to the armoury of the art: no other, except Shakespeare, has been so true, gentle, wise and merry in his statement of what is significant in life.